immersion blender and food processing recipes

MARIAN GETZ

INTRODUCTION BY WOLFGANG PUCK

MASH CHOP DICE EMULSIFY PUREE SHRED SLICE KNEAD

> AS I LEARNED LONG AGO, ALONGSIDE MY MOTHER AND GRANDMOTHER, YOU SHOULD ALWAYS PUT LOTS OF LOVE INTO EVERYTHING YOU COOK. THIS IS CERTAINLY EVIDENT IN THIS COOKBOOK.

Wolfgang Puck

The modern tools we have in the kitchen, whether in the restaurant or at home, are expected to be able to do more than one thing. While an immersion blender is typically thought of as an appliance that can only blend ingredients, the Immersion Processor Dicer is capable of performing a variety of tasks. This kitchen tool can be used to make breakfast, lunch, dinner, sauces, dressings, drinks and more.

The Immersion Processor Dicer is the perfect multi-tasker. The different speed buttons as well as a variety of attachments allows for chopping, slicing, shredding, blending, mashing, pureeing, emulsifying and kneading ingredients with ease.

Marian was thrilled to write a cookbook to accompany this appliance. She instantly thought of dozens of recipes to include in this cookbook. Her experience as a pastry chef, wife, mother, and grandmother allowed Marian to put together a cookbook with a wide variety of recipes that I'm sure you will use for years to come.

A student of cooking is probably one of the best ways to describe Marian. She is always looking for something new, something fresh, something local, something seasonal. Her culinary knowledge combined with her passion for cooking is second to none. The recipes that Marian has written for this cookbook will motivate you to be more creative in the kitchen.

table of contents

helpful tips

The Wolfgang Puck Immersion Processor Dicer dramatically cuts down your meal prep time, allowing you to cook more often for your family. Just pop your ingredients into this appliance then tap away on the desired speed button and watch your ingredients transform effortlessly in seconds. While the recipes were written for Wolfgang Puck's Immersion Processor Dicer, you can still follow the recipes and achieve similar results using traditional prep methods.

CHOPPING BLADE

The Chopping Blade, also referred to as "S-Blade", is the most commonly used blade for prepping ingredients. Many recipes call for several produce items to be chopped before any cooking can begin, and the Chopping Blade together with the Work Bowl cuts down your prep time significantly so that you can get to cooking faster. No longer do you have to sharpen a knife or clean large cutting boards for chopping as this blade does all the chopping faster and more uniform than traditional chopping. One of the best features of using the Chopping Blade and Work Bowl to chop onions is that due to the enclosed environment, the onions will be chopped before the onion fumes can cause tears.

SHREDDER

The Shredder makes long, even strands of cheeses, carrots, zucchini and many other firm foods. If you want to make a restaurant-quality dish that includes cheese, try shredding your own from a block of cheese. Pre-shredded cheese is coated in starch and anti-caking agents that affect the taste and texture. While I certainly do use pre-shredded cheeses as a time saver and call for them in many of my recipes, shredding cheese from a block is a great way to improve the taste of your recipe.

SLICER

The Slicer makes perfectly even, thin slices of most produce. One of my favorite foods to slice is cooked, chilled chicken breasts. I could never replicate such quick, thin and uniform slices, even using the best knife.

DICER

The Dicer is the newest tool to perfectly and evenly dice fruits or vegetables. Watching them fall into the bottom of the Work Bowl after being diced in seconds is mesmerizing and makes your dishes look professional. Wolfgang's favorite vegetable to dice is cucumber to make cucumber salad as he loves the texture and uniform look of the small cucumber squares.

BLENDING ROD

The Blending Rod is my favorite of all the attachments. It is incredibly fast as well as easy and intuitive to use. This attachment "goes to the food" instead of the "food coming to it" which is the case with most other blending appliances. Its small size also makes it easy to store and clean. When a kitchen appliance fits all those criteria, it quickly becomes my trusted companion in the kitchen. It is also the best secret weapon for instantly getting lumps out of gravy.

WIRE WHISK

The Wire Whisk is used to aerate foods such as your morning hot milk for coffee, eggs for an omelet or whipped cream. It's great to use with the Mixing Beaker which contains the food well and prevents most ingredients from splashing out due to its tall shape. However, if you are using it to whip cream, cover the opening partially with a paper towel as cream creates just about the most splatter of any food that is being whipped.

MASHER

The Masher will get you rave reviews the next time you use it to make the creamiest, silkiest mashed potatoes. The non-sharp blade with its slower spin than those of a traditional mixer is the secret to the amazing mashing performance. The starch granules in potatoes quickly become sticky or unpleasantly "gluey" when mixing or mashing too fast using a machine with a sharp blade. For best results, mash in a straight-sided pot that is only half full of ingredients. Pass the Masher over a pile or "stack" of potatoes in the pot then pull up and reposition over the next pile. It takes just seconds to pass through a whole pot full of boiled potatoes using this attachment.

THE HOPPER

The Hopper is designed to hold items to be processed upright and feed the cutting blades with the ingredients at an optimal angle to produce thin and even cuts. The Hopper can also be used as an opening to add ingredients while the machine is in operation, such as pouring olive oil into a dressing as it emulsifies. It may be necessary to cut some ingredients into smaller chunks to fit inside the Hopper. If the item is relatively small, such as baby potatoes, it should fit without having to cut it. Medium sized foods, such as tomatoes, can most likely be quartered while larger foods, such as large onions, will need to be cut into chunks to comfortably fit inside the Hopper. Always use the Food Pusher when pushing foods through the Hopper. The textured bottom of the Food Pusher will grip the food and aid in feeding them through the Hopper. This will ensure consistently sliced, diced or shredded ingredients while keeping your fingers away from moving blades.

MIXING BEAKER

The Mixing Beaker contains foods so well, it is perfect for using it with the Blending Rod or Wire Whisk as its tall and narrow shape prevents spilling. You can also use it as a large measuring cup because of the measuring marks on the side of the Mixing Beaker.

SPEED SETTINGS

The difference between the HIGH and LOW button of your appliance is the speed at which the blades turn. Start by using the LOW setting until you get a feel for how the machine operates. Once you are comfortable, start using the HIGH setting. As you become more familiar with the appliance, you will most likely use the HIGH speed for the majority of recipes. I mostly use the LOW speed when chopping ingredients to a chunky texture such as salsa and use the HIGH speed when turning ingredients creamy and smooth such as soup. You can use either speed for most of the recipes unless specifically stated. Many recipes also call for "pulsing" which means tapping either speed button for a number of times. This prevents ingredients from being over-processed.

OVERFILLING

Try not to fill the Work Bowl more than half full of ingredients whenever possible as they might not get chopped evenly when using the Chopping Blade. If you overfill the Work Bowl, the ingredients at the bottom tend to get chopped faster than the ingredients on top, resulting in inconsistent chopping. When using the Mixing Beaker, try not to fill it more than half full to prevent ingredients from spilling out when using with the Wire Whisk or Blending Rod.

OVERMIXING

Watch closely when using your Immersion Processor Dicer as its fast speed and powerful motor can potentially overmix your ingredients. To monitor the progress during chopping, it's best to tilt your head and view the Work Bowl from eye level then stop chopping when your desired consistency is achieved. I like to watch the ingredients I am processing closely to ensure that they are mixed just right. This applies to all the attachments except the Dicer, Slicer and Shredder. Once the food has passed through either one of those three attachments, they will not be processed any further as they fall to the bottom of the Work Bowl.

CLEANING

For general cleaning, add 2 inches of warm water and a small amount of dish soap to the Work Bowl then cover and blend on either speed to let the power of the appliance do the cleaning for you. Simply rinse with clean water and dry before storing. You can also use a small brush similar to those created for cleaning baby bottles. It is a very helpful tool to remove even the smallest seeds. Other parts such as the Blending Rod, Masher and Wire Whisk can be placed inside another vessel with water and dish soap then turned on to let the motor do the cleaning. Please see additional cleaning instructions in the product manual.

pantry tips

Being prepared to cook the recipes in this book, or any recipe for that matter, is one of the keys to success in the kitchen. Your pantry must be stocked with the basics. We all know how frustrating it can be when you go to the cupboard and what you need is not there. This list includes some ingredients you will find in this book and some that we feel are important to always have on hand.

PERISHABLES	DRY GOODS	SPICES	DAIRY
Cilantro	Flour	Salt	Butter
Onions	Gluten-Free Baking Mix	Pepper	Heavy Cream
Garlic	Honey	Mustard	Milk
Ginger	Yeast	Vinegars	Cheeses
Potatoes	Bread	Oils	Eggs
Celery	Raisins	Cooking Spray	Sour Cream
Citrus	Pineapple	Paprika	
Mushrooms	Sugar	Bay Leaves	
Carrots	Olives	Oregano	
Avocado	Capers	Cinnamon	
Salad Greens	Dates	Cream of Tartar	
Broccoli	Wine	Baking Soda	
Cauliflower	Condensed Milk	Baking Powder	
Cucumber	Soy Sauce	Vanilla Extract	
Chives	Nuts		
Cabbages	Ketchup		
Bell Peppers	Pasta		
Tomatoes	Rice		
Zucchini	Pasta Sauce		
Yellow Squash	Tortillas/Chips		
Chiles	Chocolate		
	Hot Sauce		
	Pickles/Relish		

It is not necessary to have all the items listed at all times. However, if you are feeling creative, adventurous or just following a recipe, it's great to have a good selection in the kitchen.

fresh
salsa

Makes 2 cups

12 campari tomatoes

1/4 medium white onion

2 serrano chiles, halved, or to taste

1 whole garlic clove

Handful fresh cilantro

Zest and juice of 2 limes

Kosher salt to taste

Tortilla chips, for serving

1 Fit Chopping Blade in Work Bowl, add all ingredients, except tortilla chips, then secure Lid and attach Motor.

2 Pulse for 15 seconds until desired consistency is achieved.

3 When processing is complete, remove and serve with tortilla chips.

4 Salsa keeps in an airtight container in the refrigerator for up to 3 days.

mashed potatoes

Makes 6 servings

4 pounds Russet or sweet potatoes, peeled and chunked

Water, as needed

Kosher salt to taste

Unsalted butter to taste

1/2 cup to 1 1/2 cups whole milk, or as needed

1. Place potatoes into a large pot then add water until potatoes are covered by 1-inch of water.

2. Place pot over medium-high heat then add salt and bring to a boil.

3. As soon as water is boiling, reduce heat to a simmer.

4. Cook for 20-30 minutes or until potatoes are fork tender then drain thoroughly.

5. Attach Masher to Motor.

6. Add butter to the potatoes then mash until smooth.

7. When mashing is complete, stir in enough milk using a spatula until desired texture is achieved.

8. Garnish as desired and serve hot.

everything bagel cheese boats

Makes 4 boats

- 8 sticks of string cheese
- 4 ounces Swiss cheese, cubed
- 4 ounces cream cheese, softened
- 2 whole garlic cloves
- Kosher salt and fresh pepper to taste
- All purpose flour, as needed
- 1 ball store-bought pizza dough (1 pound)
- 1 large egg, beaten
- 2 tablespoons everything bagel seasoning

1 Line a sheet pan with parchment paper and set aside.

2 Fit Chopping Blade in Work Bowl, add string cheese, Swiss cheese, cream cheese, garlic, salt and pepper, then secure Lid and attach Motor.

3 Process for 30 seconds or until uniform in texture then set aside.

4 On an floured surface, divide pizza dough into 4 equal pieces, roll each piece into an oval then place on the prepared sheet pan.

5 Press down the center of each oval then place 1/4 of the cheese mixture in the center of each oval.

6 Pinch and pull up the edges then gently press down the cheese mixture.

7 Brush edges with beaten egg then sprinkle with some bagel seasoning.

8 Cover loosely with plastic wrap and let rise for 25 minutes or until doubled in bulk.

9 Preheat oven to 350°F while dough is rising.

10 Bake for 15-20 minutes or until golden brown and cheese is melted.

11 When baking is complete, remove and serve hot.

chinois chicken salad

Makes 4 servings

For the Salad:

1 Napa cabbage head

2 garlic ginger chicken breasts, cooked and cooled (see recipe on page 57)

1 red bell pepper, julienned

1 cup snow peas

1 carrot, julienned

1 can (3 ounces) rice noodles, for serving

For the Dressing:

1 tablespoon dry mustard

1/3 cup rice vinegar

2 tablespoons soy sauce

Kosher salt to taste

1 tablespoon sesame oil

3 tablespoons honey

1/2 cup vegetable oil

1   Fit Slicer in Work Bowl, secure Lid then attach Motor.

2   Stand as many cabbage leaves as will fit inside the Hopper and process until sliced.

3   Repeat with remaining cabbage then transfer to a serving bowl.

4   Cut chicken to fit inside the Hopper, process until sliced, transfer to the serving bowl with the cabbage then add the bell peppers, snow peas and carrots.

5   In a small bowl, whisk together all dressing ingredients until smooth.

6   Pour dressing over the salad in the serving bowl and toss well.

7   Top with rice noodles and serve.

easy hummus

Makes 1 1/2 cups

1 can (15 ounces) chickpeas, drained + more for topping

1/4 cup tahini

2 tablespoons olive oil + more for serving

1/4 cup fresh lemon juice

2 whole garlic cloves

Kosher salt to taste

1/4 cup water

Paprika, for serving

Dippers of your choice, for serving

1 In a microwave-safe bowl, microwave chickpeas for 1-2 minutes or until hot.

2 Fit Chopping Blade in Work Bowl, add chickpeas and remaining ingredients, except paprika and dippers, then secure Lid and attach Motor.

3 Process for 2 minutes or until hummus is mostly smooth.

4 When processing is complete, transfer to a serving bowl, sprinkle with additional chickpeas, olive oil and paprika then serve with desired dippers.

gluten-free pizza dough

Makes 1 pizza crust

1 1/2 cups gluten-free baking mix
1/4 teaspoon kosher salt
1/2 cup water

1 teaspoon olive oil
1 teaspoon honey
1 envelope (1/4 ounce) active dry yeast

1   Fit Chopping Blade in Work Bowl, add gluten-free baking mix and salt then secure Lid and attach Motor.

2   Process for 5 seconds to combine.

3   In a measuring cup, combine remaining ingredients.

4   With the motor running, pour mixture through the Hopper and process for 30 seconds or until mixture looks like cake batter.

5   Scrape mixture into an oiled bowl, cover with plastic wrap and let rise at room temperature for 30 minutes.

6   Using additional baking mix, gently pat dough ball into a 10-inch circle. Please note that this dough is very soft and does not stretch like other pizza dough.

7   Top as desired then bake at 450°F for 10-12 minutes or until crust is brown.

8   Remove and serve.

individual meat loaves

Makes 4 individual loaves

1 small yellow onion, chunked
1 package (8 ounces) white mushrooms
1/2 teaspoon fresh thyme leaves
1 large egg
1/3 cup milk
3 white bread slices, torn

1 teaspoon kosher salt
1/2 teaspoon freshly ground pepper
1/2 pound ground beef
1/2 pound ground pork
12 bacon slices, raw

1 Preheat oven to 375°F and line a sheet pan with parchment paper; set aside.

2 Fit Chopping Blade in Work Bowl, add all ingredients, except beef, pork and bacon, then secure Lid and attach Motor.

3 Pulse 20 times or until mixture is semi-smooth, transfer to a large mixing bowl then stir in the beef and pork until combined.

4 Divide and shape mixture into four ovals, wrap each with three slices of bacon then place seam-side down on prepared sheet pan.

5 Bake for 25-30 minutes or until internal temperature registers 165°F on a meat thermometer.

6 When baking is complete, remove, garnish as desired and serve.

easy mayonnaise

Makes 2 cups

2 large eggs

2 teaspoons kosher salt

1 tablespoon dry mustard powder

1 tablespoon white vinegar

2 cups vegetable oil

1. Attach Blending Rod to Motor.

2. Place all ingredients into the Mixing Beaker.

3. Position the Blending Rod all the way at the bottom of the Mixing Beaker, making sure that both egg yolks are positioned under the head of the Blending Rod.

4. While holding the Blending Rod in place at the bottom of the Mixing Beaker, blend on HIGH speed for 30 seconds or until mayonnaise is forming at the bottom of the Mixing Beaker.

5. While continuing to blend, slowly raise the Blending Rod to the top until all ingredients are incorporated into the mayonnaise.

6. When blending is complete, transfer to an airtight storage container.

7. Keeps refrigerated for up to 1 week.

carrot raisin salad

Makes 4 servings

For the Salad:
4 large carrots, peeled
1/4 cup raisins
1/4 cup canned pineapple tidbits

For the Dressing:
1/2 cup mayonnaise
2 tablespoons granulated sugar
2 tablespoons yellow mustard
Kosher salt to taste

1 Fit Shredder in Work Bowl, secure Lid then attach Motor.

2 Fit as many carrots as will fit inside the Hopper and process until shredded.

3 Repeat with remaining carrots then transfer to a serving bowl.

4 Add raisins and pineapple to the carrots.

5 In a small bowl, whisk together all dressing ingredients until smooth.

6 Pour dressing over the serving bowl contents and toss well.

7 Garnish as desired and serve.

easy guacamole

Makes 8 servings

1 small yellow onion, chunked

1 handful fresh cilantro

1 jalapeño pepper, halved (optional)

1 Fresno chile, or to taste

Zest and juice of 2 limes

Pinch of salt

4 ripe avocados, pitted and skinned

1   Fit Chopping Blade in Work Bowl, add all ingredients, except avocados, then secure Lid and attach Motor.

2   Process for 30 seconds or until fairly smooth then set aside.

3   Place avocados into a mixing bowl.

4   Attach Masher to Motor.

5   Mash avocados until smooth.

6   Using a spatula, stir the Work Bowl contents into the mashed avocados until uniform.

7   Serve as desired.

Marian's Tip: *When buying avocados, make sure that the stem is intact or air will get inside which can cause them to darken prematurely.*

egg
salad

Makes 2 1/2 cups

4 gherkin sweet pickles

1 small dill pickle

1 small wedge yellow onion

Kosher salt and fresh pepper to taste

6 hard boiled eggs

2 teaspoons granulated sugar

2 tablespoons yellow mustard

2 teaspoons lemon juice

1/2 cup mayonnaise

2 tablespoons unsalted butter, softened

Soft bread, for serving

1 Fit Chopping Blade in Work Bowl, add both kinds of pickles and onion, then secure Lid and attach Motor.

2 Pulse 10 times or until pieces are small.

3 Add remaining ingredients, except bread, then pulse until texture is just chunky.

4 Spread on soft bread, garnish as desired and serve.

chicken marbella

Makes 3-6 servings

6 whole garlic cloves

1 handful fresh oregano leaves

4 tablespoons olive oil

4 tablespoons red wine vinegar

1 cup raisins

6 tablespoons capers

6 chicken pieces, raw, skin scored

1 cup green olives

2 bay leaves

Kosher salt and fresh pepper to taste

1/2 cup white wine

8 small potatoes

1 carrot, sliced

1 cup peas, frozen

1 Attach Blending Rod to Motor.

2 Place the garlic, oregano, oil and red wine vinegar into the Mixing Beaker.

3 Blend for 10 seconds or until pieces are small.

4 Place Mixing Beaker contents and remaining ingredients, except peas, into a large plastic zipper top bag then refrigerate for a minimum of 2 hours or up to 24 hours.

5 Preheat oven to 400°F, line a sheet pan with parchment paper or aluminum foil then pour bag contents evenly across the prepared sheet pan.

6 Bake for 30-40 minutes or until chicken is brown on top and internal temperature of chicken pieces registers 165°F on a meat thermometer.

7 Add peas, bake for an additional 5 minutes then remove and serve hot.

This recipe works with any piece of chicken. Scoring the surface of the chicken helps the flavors infuse better. For additional flavor, add a handful of oregano sprigs to the sheet pan before baking.

Marian's Tip:

key lime pie

Makes one pie

3 packages (8 ounces each) cream cheese, softened

1 can (14 ounces) sweetened condensed milk

1/2 cup lime juice

2-3 drops green food coloring (optional)

Zest from 2 limes + more for serving

1 store-bought graham cracker crust

Whipped cream, for topping
(see recipe on next page)

1 Fit Chopping Blade in Work Bowl, add cream cheese then secure Lid and attach Motor.

2 Process for 1 minute, scraping down the sides of the Work Bowl as needed.

3 Add the condensed milk, lime juice, food coloring and zest then process for an additional 30 seconds or until smooth. Scrape down the sides of the Work Bowl as needed.

4 Using a spatula, scrape the mixture into the graham cracker crust then smooth the top.

5 Top with whipped cream, cover and refrigerate for a minimum of 2 hours or up to 24 hours then garnish with additional lime zest before serving.

whipped cream

Makes 4 cups

2 cups heavy cream, cold
1/2 cup powdered sugar or other sweetener
1/2 teaspoon vanilla extract

1 Attach Wire Whisk to Motor.

2 Pour the cream, powdered sugar and vanilla into the Mixing Beaker.

3 Whip mixture for 1 minute or until medium peaks form.

4 Use as desired.

cantaloupe sorbet

Makes 4 servings

1 ripe cantaloupe, seeded and chunked
1/2 cup granulated sugar or other sweetener
1/4 cup light corn syrup

Zest and juice of 1 lemon
Pinch of kosher salt

1 Fit Chopping Blade in Work Bowl, add all ingredients then secure Lid and attach Motor.

2 Process for 1 minute or until smooth.

3 When processing is complete, transfer mixture to a freezer-safe lidded container.

4 Place in freezer until semi-frozen (do not freeze into a solid block).

5 Remove from freezer, return to the Work Bowl and pulse until slushy in texture.

6 Garnish as desired and serve immediately.

s'mores no churn ice cream

Makes 6 servings

2 cups mini marshmallows

2 cups heavy cream, cold

1 can (14 ounces) sweetened condensed milk

1 teaspoon vanilla extract

1/2 cup jarred chocolate fudge sauce

2 cups bear-shaped graham crackers

1 Preheat broiler then place marshmallows on a sheet pan.

2 Broil for 2-3 minutes or until marshmallows are browned to your liking; set aside.

3 Attach Wire Whisk to Motor then pour the heavy cream into the Mixing Beaker.

4 Whip cream for 30 seconds or until soft peaks form.

5 Stir condensed milk and vanilla into the cream using a spatula.

6 In a freezer-safe container, layer cream mixture, marshmallows, chocolate sauce and crackers then cover with a lid.

7 Freeze for a minimum of 4 hours or up to 24 hours before serving.

chicken lettuce cups

Makes 4 servings

6 fresh ginger coins

6 whole garlic cloves

1 bunch green onions, chunked

1 package (8 ounces) white mushrooms

2 tablespoons sesame oil

1 pound ground chicken

3 tablespoons hoisin sauce

Kosher salt and fresh pepper to taste

Lettuce cups, as needed

Julienned carrots, red bell peppers, snow peas and crispy rice noodles, for serving

1   Fit Chopping Blade in Work Bowl, add ginger, garlic, green onions and mushrooms then secure Lid and attach Motor.

2   Pulse 20 times or until pieces are small.

3   Preheat the oil in large skillet over medium-high heat.

4   Add the Work Bowl contents and chicken to the skillet then cook while stirring constantly until chicken is cooked through.

5   Add hoisin sauce, salt and pepper to the skillet then stir until heated through.

6   Divide mixture between lettuce cups then serve with carrots, bell peppers, snow peas and crispy rice noodles.

potato latkes

Makes 4 servings

2 pounds Russet potatoes, chunked
1 small yellow onion, chunked
Kosher salt and fresh pepper to taste

2 large eggs
Vegetable oil, for frying
Sour cream and apple sauce, for serving

1 Fit Shredder in Work Bowl, secure Lid then attach Motor.

2 Fit as many potatoes and onions as will fit inside the Hopper and process until shredded.

3 Repeat with remaining potatoes and onions.

4 Remove the shredded potatoes and onions, squeeze out all the liquid using your hands or paper towels then return to the Work Bowl and add salt, pepper and eggs; stir to combine using a spoon.

5 Preheat a large skillet over medium-high heat then add enough oil to cover the bottom of the skillet.

6 Drop spoonfuls of potato mixture into the skillet and fry for 3 minutes on each side or until brown and crispy.

7 Remove and drain on paper towels, repeat with remaining potato mixture then serve with sour cream and apple sauce.

bacon cheddar pretzel dip

Makes 4-6 servings

1/4 cup lager-style beer

1 bunch green onions + more for garnish

3 whole garlic cloves

1 teaspoon hot sauce, or to taste

1 package (3.5 ounces) cooked, chopped bacon

Kosher salt and fresh pepper to taste

1 cup Cheddar cheese, shredded

1 package (8 ounces) cream cheese, softened

Pretzel bites, for serving

1 Fit Chopping Blade in Work Bowl, add all ingredients, except pretzel bites, then secure Lid and attach Motor.

2 Process for 30 seconds or until desired texture is achieved.

3 When processing is complete, transfer to a shallow oven-safe baking dish and broil for 3-5 minutes or until brown and bubbly. Alternatively, you can microwave in a microwave-safe dish for 3-5 minutes or until bubbly.

4 Top with additional green onions and serve with pretzel bites.

ranch hash brown potatoes

Makes 4 servings

1 1/2 pounds baby gold or red potatoes

1 small yellow onion, chunked

3 tablespoons vegetable oil

1 package (1 ounce) dry ranch dressing mix, or to taste

1 tablespoon unsalted butter

Fresh pepper to taste

1 tablespoon fresh parsley, chopped

1 Fit Dicer in Work Bowl, secure Lid then attach Motor.

2 Fit as many potatoes and onions as will fit inside the Hopper and process until diced.

3 Repeat with remaining potatoes and onions.

4 Preheat a large skillet over medium-high heat then add the oil.

5 Add potatoes and onions to the skillet then shake into an even layer.

6 Cook for 5-6 minutes, stirring frequently, or until beginning to brown on all sides.

7 Sprinkle Ranch dressing mix over skillet contents then add remaining ingredients, except parsley.

8 Cook for an additional 5-6 minutes, stirring frequently, or until well browned and crispy.

9 When cooking is complete, drain on paper towels, garnish with parsley and serve.

vegetarian broccoli sushi rolls

Makes 6 rolls

1/2 small broccoli head, cut into florets

1/2 small cauliflower head, cut into florets

2 tablespoons store-bought toasted sesame seeds

1 tablespoon seasoned rice vinegar

2 tablespoons mayonnaise

2 teaspoons sriracha hot sauce, or to taste

6 nori sheets

1 avocado, sliced

1 cucumber, thinly sliced

1 carrot, julienned

1 red bell pepper, julienned

Soy sauce, wasabi and pickled ginger, for serving

1 Fit Chopping Blade in Work Bowl, add broccoli and cauliflower then secure Lid and attach Motor.

2 Pulse 20 times or until vegetables are the size of rice.

3 Transfer Work Bowl contents to a mixing bowl then stir in sesame seeds, rice vinegar, mayonnaise and sriracha.

4 Place a nori sheet on the counter then top evenly with a layer of broccoli mixture.

5 Starting at one side of the nori sheet, form a line with avocado slices, cucumber slices, carrots and bell peppers.

6 Carefully roll up the nori sheet into a sushi roll then place seam-side down on a cutting board.

7 Repeat to make additional rolls.

8 Cut each roll into 8 equal pieces and serve with soy sauce, wasabi and pickled ginger.

9 If you have any broccoli mixture left over, you can serve as a side dish or in a salad. Mixture keeps for up to 2 days in the refrigerator.

Marian's Tip: *For a low carb non-vegetarian version, you can fill these sushi rolls with shrimp, crab or even imitation crab. You can also add or omit any vegetable according to your personal taste.*

pesto
pasta

Makes 4 servings

1/4 cup pine nuts

3 cups basil leaves, slightly packed

1/4 cup Parmesan cheese, grated

Kosher salt to taste

5 whole garlic cloves

1 cup olive oil

1 pound hot pasta, cooked

1 Fit Chopping Blade in Work Bowl, add all ingredients, except oil and pasta, then secure Lid and attach Motor.

2 Process for 30 seconds then continue processing while slowly pouring the oil through the Hopper until mostly smooth.

3 Pour 1/2 cup pesto over hot pasta, toss to combine and serve.

4 Keep leftover pesto in an airtight storage container in the refrigerator for up to 1 week or in the freezer for up to 2 months.

Marian's Tip: *If using the pesto for sautéing in a hot pan, omit the cheese to prevent sticking then add it at the end. If you would like to save calories, you can substitute 1 cup olive oil with a mixture of 1/2 cup water + 1/2 cup olive oil.*

glazed salmon
with edamame

Makes 4 servings

For the Glaze:

4 whole garlic cloves

4 fresh ginger coins

3 green onions

1/4 cup soy sauce

1/4 cup honey

2 tablespoons olive oil

For the Salmon:

4 salmon fillets

2 cups edamame, shelled

Kosher salt and fresh pepper to taste

1 Attach Blending Rod to Motor.

2 Place all glaze ingredients into the Mixing Beaker.

3 Blend until glaze is mostly smooth.

4 Preheat a large skillet over medium-high heat then pour the glaze into the skillet.

5 When glaze begins to bubble, add the salmon to the skillet and cook for 3-4 minutes.

6 Flip salmon over, arrange the edamame around the salmon, season with salt and pepper then cook for an additional 2-3 minutes or until salmon is cooked to your desired doneness.

7 When cooking is complete, remove, garnish as desired and serve.

broccoli tots

Makes 6 servings

1 large fresh broccoli head, cut into chunks
4 green onions + more for garnishing
2 whole garlic cloves
1 cup Cheddar cheese, shredded

1 large egg
1 cup panko breadcrumbs
Kosher salt and fresh pepper to taste
Ketchup, for serving

1   Preheat oven to 400°F and line a sheet pan with parchment paper; set aside.

2   Fit Chopping Blade in Work Bowl, add broccoli, green onions and garlic then secure Lid and attach Motor.

3   Process for 10-15 seconds or until pieces are small.

4   Add remaining ingredients, except ketchup, then pulse to combine.

5   Using a teaspoon and your fingers, shape mixture into tots then place onto the prepared sheet pan.

6   Bake for 10-20 minutes then carefully turn each tot over using tongs and bake for an additional 10-20 minutes or until brown and crispy.

7   Remove, garnish with additional green onions and serve with ketchup.

stovetop
mac and cheese

Makes 4 servings

4 cups whole milk

2 tablespoons unsalted butter

Kosher salt to taste

1 teaspoon Dijon mustard

3 cups (12 ounces) small pasta shells, uncooked

1 block (8 ounces) sharp Cheddar cheese

5 sticks of string cheese

1   In a large saucepan over medium-high heat, bring the milk, butter, salt, mustard and pasta to a boil.

2   Reduce heat to a simmer and stir frequently for about 10 minutes or until pasta is tender (do not drain).

3   While pasta is simmering, fit Shredder in Work Bowl, secure Lid then attach Motor.

4   Fit as much cheese as will fit inside the Hopper and process until shredded.

5   Repeat until both cheeses are shredded.

6   Add cheeses to undrained pasta, stir until melted and serve.

low carb pizza

Makes 1 pizza

For the Crust:

1 cauliflower head, cut into florets

1/2 cup mozzarella cheese, shredded

1/4 cup Parmesan cheese, grated

1/2 teaspoon dried oregano

1/2 teaspoon garlic powder

2 large eggs

For Topping:

1/2 cup jarred pasta sauce

1 cup mozzarella cheese, shredded

1/2 cup Parmesan cheese, grated

1/2 cup mini pepperoni slices

2 teaspoons oregano, chopped

1. Preheat oven to 400°F and line a sheet pan or pizza pan with parchment paper; set aside.

2. Fit Chopping Blade in Work Bowl, add cauliflower then secure Lid and attach Motor.

3. Pulse 5-10 times or until pieces are small then add remaining crust ingredients and pulse a few times just until combined.

4. Transfer Work Bowl contents onto the prepared pan, pat into a thin crust then bake in the center of the oven for 20-25 minutes or until beginning to brown.

5. Carefully top crust with all topping ingredients in the order listed then bake for an additional 10-15 minutes or until brown and bubbly.

6. When baking is complete, remove, garnish as desired and serve.

shrimp scampi burgers

Makes 4 servings

1 pounds shrimp, peeled and deveined

2 whole garlic cloves

4 green onions, roughly chopped

Kosher salt and fresh pepper to taste

2 tablespoons fresh lemon juice

2 tablespoons unsalted butter

Buns and condiments of your choice, for serving

1   Fit Chopping Blade in Work Bowl, add shrimp, garlic, green onions, salt, pepper and lemon juice then secure Lid and attach Motor.

2   Pulse 12-15 times or until pieces are small.

3   Gently pat mixture into 4 equal patties.

4   Preheat a large skillet over medium heat then add the butter.

5   Add the patties to the skillet and cook for 2-3 minutes on each side or until patties are firm and pink all the way through.

6   Remove patties, place on buns and serve with condiments of your choice.

jalapeño popper dip

Makes 8 servings

3 whole garlic cloves

1 cup mayonnaise

1 cup Parmesan cheese, shredded

1 cup Monterey Jack cheese, shredded

Kosher salt and fresh pepper to taste

1 bunch green onions, roughly chopped

6 jalapeño peppers or to taste

Dippers of your choice, for serving

1 Preheat oven to 350°F and apply nonstick cooking spray to a shallow baking dish; set aside.

2 Fit Chopping Blade in Work Bowl, add garlic, mayonnaise, cheeses, salt and pepper then secure Lid and attach Motor.

3 Process for 30 seconds or until smooth.

4 Add the green onions and jalapeño peppers then pulse until pieces are small.

5 Transfer mixture to the prepared baking dish then bake for 30 minutes or until brown and bubbly. Alternatively, transfer mixture to a microwave-safe dish and microwave for 5-6 minutes or until hot and bubbly.

6 When baking is complete, remove, garnish as desired and serve with dippers of your choice.

If you don't like or can't have spicy foods, use one drained jar (4 ounces) of diced, red pimentos instead of the jalapeño peppers for a similar flavor without the heat.

Marian's Tip:

41

apple gelatin dessert

Makes 6 servings

1/4 cup cold water

3 packages (1/4 ounce each) unflavored gelatin

4 cups apple juice

1/4 cup granulated sugar or other sweetener

2 tablespoons lemon juice

3 large Granny Smith apples, chunked

1 Apply a thin layer of nonstick cooking spray to an 8-cup mold or bowl; set aside.

2 In a microwave-safe bowl, whisk together the water and gelatin; let stand for 5 minutes to soften.

3 Microwave gelatin mixture for 30-40 seconds or until clear.

4 In a separate mixing bowl, stir together the apple juice, sugar and lemon juice then stir in hot gelatin mixture.

5 Pour mixture into prepared mold or bowl; set aside.

6 Fit Dicer in Work Bowl, secure Lid then attach Motor.

7 Fit as many apples as will fit inside the Hopper then process until diced.

8 Repeat with remaining apples.

9 Stir diced apples into the gelatin mixture (they will float to the top) then refrigerate for a minimum of 4 hours or up to 24 hours.

10 Invert onto a serving platter to unmold and serve.

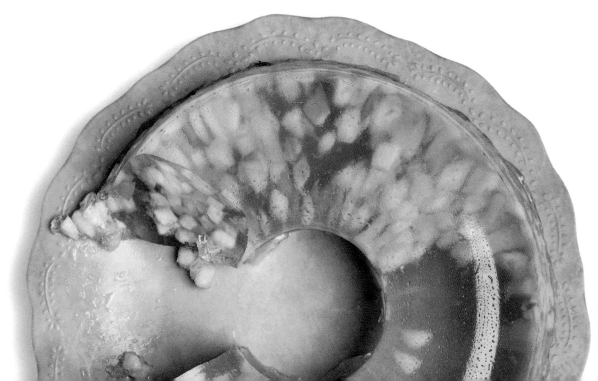

classic
pie crust

Makes 1 crust

1/4 cup unsalted butter, cold and cubed

1/4 cup solid white shortening, cold

1 1/2 cups all purpose flour

1/2 teaspoon kosher salt

1 teaspoon apple cider vinegar

2 tablespoons ice water, or as needed

1 Fit Chopping Blade in Work Bowl, add butter, shortening, flour and salt then secure Lid and attach Motor.

2 Pulse 5-10 times or until the butter is the size of small peas.

3 While continuing to pulse, pour the vinegar and enough of the ice water through the Hopper just until a dough ball forms (if dough seems dry, add water, 1 teaspoon at a time, until a dough ball forms).

4 Remove dough, shape into a disc, wrap in plastic wrap then chill for a minimum of 1 hour or up to 3 days.

5 Preheat oven to 350°F and apply nonstick baking spray to a pie pan.

6 Roll out dough, place in pie pan then top with a sheet of parchment paper.

7 To hold crust in place, fill pie pan to the top with granulated sugar, bake for 30 minutes then remove parchment and sugar (and reserve sugar for another use).

8 Bake crust for an additional 5 minutes or until golden brown then remove and use as desired.

ombre orange cheesecake

Makes one cake

For the Crust:

2 sleeves graham crackers

2/3 cup unsalted butter, melted

For the Filling:

1 pound cream cheese, softened

1/4 cup orange juice

1 teaspoon orange extract

1 can (14 ounces) sweetened condensed milk

1 teaspoon vanilla extract

Orange food coloring

1 Fit Chopping Blade in Work Bowl, add graham crackers, breaking them up to fit, then secure Lid and attach Motor.

2 Process for 20 seconds or until finely ground.

3 Add butter then pulse just until incorporated.

4 Transfer cracker mixture to an oiled 6-inch springform pan then pat into an even layer to cover the bottom of the pan; set aside.

5 Rinse out the Work Bowl and Chopping Blade.

6 Place all filling ingredients, except food coloring, into the Work Bowl then secure Lid and attach Motor.

7 Process for 20 seconds or until mostly smooth.

8 Divide mixture between 4 mixing bowls.

9 To the first mixing bowl, add 4 drops orange food coloring or until pale in color.

10 Double the amount of food coloring with each of the next 3 mixing bowls until you have 4 different shades of orange.

11 Pour darkest color over cracker layer in the pan then freeze for 10 minutes or until firm.

12 Repeat with each additional color, freezing until firm in between each layer.

13 Cover and refrigerate for a minimum of 4 hours or up to 24 hours.

14 Garnish as desired and serve.

bread and butter pickles

Makes 1-quart

For the Vegetables:

2 English cucumbers

1 small yellow onion, chunked

For the Brine:

1 cup white vinegar

2 tablespoons kosher salt or to taste

1/2 cup granulated sugar or other sweetener

2 tablespoons pickling spice

1/4 teaspoon ground tumeric

1 Fit Slicer in Work Bowl, secure Lid then attach Motor.

2 Fit as many vegetables as will fit inside the Hopper and process until sliced.

3 Repeat until all vegetables are sliced then transfer to a lidded storage container.

4 Attach Wire Whisk to Motor, pour all brine ingredients into the Mixing Beaker then whisk for 5 seconds or until salt and sugar are dissolved.

5 Pour brine over the vegetables in the storage container (not all vegetables need to be submerged).

6 Let container stand for 10 minutes, shake or invert container to evenly distribute the brine then let stand for an additional 10 minutes before serving.

7 Store in the refrigerator for up to 2 weeks.

brussels sprouts slaw salad

Makes 4 servings

For the Slaw:

1 pound Brussels sprouts, trimmed

1/2 cup dried cranberries

1/2 cup almonds, slivered

1/2 cup Parmesan cheese, grated

1 can (4 ounces) Mandarin oranges, drained

For the Dressing:

2 tablespoons white vinegar

3 tablespoons honey

2 tablespoons brown mustard

1/4 cup olive oil

Kosher salt and fresh pepper to taste

1 Fit Slicer in Work Bowl, secure Lid then attach Motor.

2 Fit as many Brussels sprouts as will fit inside the Hopper and process until sliced.

3 Repeat with remaining Brussels sprouts then transfer to a serving bowl.

4 Top Brussels sprouts with remaining slaw ingredients.

5 Attach Wire Whisk to Motor, pour all dressing ingredients into the Mixing Beaker then whisk until smooth.

6 Pour dressing over the slaw in the serving bowl and toss well.

7 Cover and refrigerate for a minimum of 2 hours or up to 48 hours.

8 Garnish as desired and serve.

cauliflower mash-up

Makes 4 servings

1 large cauliflower head, cut into florets

1 whole garlic clove

2 tablespoons cream cheese

2 tablespoons unsalted butter

2 tablespoons Parmesan cheese, grated

Kosher salt and fresh pepper to taste

Chopped chives, for garnish

1 Fit Chopping Blade in Work Bowl, add cauliflower and garlic then secure Lid and attach Motor.

2 Pulse 20 times or until vegetables are the size of rice.

3 Transfer cauliflower mixture to a microwave-safe bowl then cover and microwave for 7-8 minutes or until tender (stir after 4 minutes).

4 Return cauliflower mixture to the Work Bowl then add remaining ingredients, except chives.

5 Process for an additional 1 minute or until fairly smooth then transfer to a serving dish.

6 Top with chives, garnish as desired and serve.

apple coleslaw

Makes 4 servings

For the Slaw:

1/2 small green cabbage head, chunked

1/8 small purple cabbage head, chunked

1 carrot

1 tart apple, chunked

1/4 cup raisins

For the Dressing:

2 tablespoons apple cider vinegar

1/2 cup mayonnaise

Kosher salt and fresh pepper to taste

2 tablespoons honey

1 tablespoon dijon mustard

1 Fit Slicer in Work Bowl, secure Lid then attach Motor.

2 Fit as much green and purple cabbage as will fit inside the Hopper and process until sliced.

3 Repeat with remaining cabbage then transfer to a serving bowl.

4 Fit Shredder in Work Bowl, secure Lid then attach Motor.

5 Fit carrot and as many apples as will fit inside the Hopper and process until shredded.

6 Attach Wire Whisk to Motor, pour all dressing ingredients into the Mixing Beaker then whisk until smooth.

7 Pour dressing over the slaw in the mixing bowl and toss well.

8 Top with raisins before serving.

easy bacon biscuits

Makes 8 servings

1 1/2 cups all purpose flour	1 1/4 cups heavy cream
1 teaspoon sugar	1 bag (3.5 ounces) cooked, chopped bacon
2 teaspoons baking powder	1/2 cup Parmesan cheese, shredded
1 teaspoon kosher salt	1/4 teaspoon ground tumeric (optional)

1. Preheat oven to 375°F and line a sheet pan with parchment paper; set aside.

2. Fit Chopping Blade in Work Bowl, add all ingredients, except 1 tablespoon of chopped bacon, then secure Lid and attach Motor.

3. Pulse 10-15 times or until a dough ball forms.

4. Using an ice cream scoop, divide dough into 8 even balls, place on prepared sheet pan then gently pat down the top of each dough ball using your palm.

5. Top with reserved chopped bacon.

6. Bake for 20-25 minutes or until puffed and brown.

7. When baking is complete, remove and serve hot.

Marian's Tip: *To make these biscuits gluten-free, substitute 1 1/2 cups gluten-free baking mix for the all purpose flour.*

cheesesteak sandwiches

Makes 2 sandwiches

1 1/2 bell peppers, chunked

2 large yellow onions, chunked

1 tablespoon olive oil

8 ounces beef rib eye, shaved thinly

Kosher salt and fresh pepper to taste

4 Provolone cheese slices

2 hoagie rolls, split

1. Fit Slicer in Work Bowl, secure Lid then attach Motor.

2. Fit as many bell peppers and onions as will fit inside the Hopper and process until sliced.

3. Repeat with remaining bell peppers and onions then remove and set aside.

4. Preheat the oil in a large skillet over medium-high heat.

5. Add the beef, peppers and onions to the skillet, season with salt and pepper then cook and stir frequently for 5 minutes or until beef is no longer pink.

6. Place cheese slices over skillet contents then cover skillet and let steam for 30 seconds or just until cheese is melted.

7. Divide beef mixture between hoagie rolls and serve hot.

chocolate cloud cake

Makes one 6-inch cake

4 ounces bittersweet chocolate chips

1/4 cup unsalted butter

3 large eggs

1/2 cup granulated sugar

Whipped Cream (see page 25)

Cocoa powder and chocolate shavings, for serving

1 Preheat oven to 350°F and apply nonstick baking spray to a 6-inch springform pan.

2 In a microwave-safe bowl, microwave the chocolate chips and butter until liquefied.

3 Attach Wire Whisk to Motor.

4 Pour the eggs and sugar into the Mixing Beaker.

5 Whisk for 1 minute or until tripled in volume.

6 Pour chocolate mixture into the Mixing Beaker then whisk just until uniform in color.

7 Pour into prepared baking pan then bake for 30 minutes or until puffed, dry on top and center is sunken.

8 Remove and let cool completely.

9 Top cooled cake with whipped cream, cocoa powder and chocolate shavings before serving.

Marian's Tip:
Give a flavor boost to this recipe by adding your favorite flavored liqueur. Try adding up to 2 tablespoons of orange Cointreau, raspberry Framboise or hazelnut Frangelico. Add liqueur to the eggs in step 4 before incorporating the chocolate mixture.

chocolate chip cookies

Makes 2 dozen cookies

1 cup unsalted butter, softened	2 cups all purpose flour
1 cup granulated sugar	1 teaspoon baking soda
1/2 cup light brown sugar, packed	1/2 teaspoon kosher salt
2 large eggs	1 1/2 cups chocolate chips
2 teaspoons vanilla extract	

1 Preheat oven to 350°F and line two cookie sheets with parchment paper; set aside.

2 Fit Chopping Blade in Work Bowl, add butter, both sugars, eggs and vanilla then secure Lid and attach Motor.

3 Process for 1 minute or until smooth and fluffy.

4 Add flour, baking soda and salt then pulse just until no dry ingredients are visible.

5 Stir chocolate chips into the batter using a spatula.

6 Using a small ice cream scoop, drop cookie dough onto the sheet pans, spacing them out evenly.

7 Bake for 12-15 minutes or until golden brown and slightly puffed.

8 When baking is complete, remove and repeat with any remaining dough.

9 Serve hot, warm or at room temperature.

best brownies

Makes 16 brownies

1 cup unsalted butter, softened

2 cups granulated sugar

4 large eggs

1/2 teaspoon kosher salt

1 teaspoon vanilla extract

1/2 cup cocoa powder

1 cup all purpose flour

---

1 Preheat oven to 350°F and line a 9x9-inch baking pan with parchment paper; set aside.

2 Fit Chopping Blade in Work Bowl, add butter, sugar, eggs, salt and vanilla then secure Lid and attach Motor.

3 Process for 15-20 seconds or until smooth then add remaining ingredients and pulse just until incorporated.

4 When processing is complete, transfer to the prepared baking pan.

5 Bake for 40-45 minutes or until a wooden pick inserted off-center emerges clean.

6 Remove, garnish as desired and serve hot, warm or at room temperature.

garlic ginger chicken breasts

Makes 4 servings

8 whole garlic cloves

8 fresh ginger coins

4 green onions

Handful of fresh cilantro

Chili flakes to taste

1/3 cup vegetable oil

4 chicken breasts, raw

Kosher salt to taste

1 Fit appliance with the Blending Rod.

2 Place garlic, ginger, green onions, cilantro, chili flakes and oil into the Mixing Beaker.

3 Blend for 20-30 seconds or until pieces are small.

4 Place chicken into a large plastic zipper top bag, add the garlic mixture then close the bag.

5 Let marinate in the refrigerator for a minimum of 20 minutes or up to 24 hours.

6 Preheat a large skillet over medium-high heat.

7 Transfer chicken breasts to the skillet, season with salt then cook for 8 minutes on each side or until brown and internal temperature registers 165°F on a meat thermometer.

8 When cooking is complete, remove, garnish as desired and serve. Alternatively, refrigerate for 1 hour, slice in half lengthwise to fit through the Hopper then use the Slicer and gentle pressure to cut into thin, even slices.

You can also try using this marinade to add flavor to pork chops, pork tenderloins, lamb or tofu.

Marian's Tip:

sheet pan
baked falafel

Makes 4 servings

1 can (15 ounces) chickpeas, drained

1 teaspoon baking powder

1 small yellow onion, chunked

6 whole garlic cloves

2 teaspoons ground cumin

2 teaspoons ground coriander

Bottled hot sauce, to taste

1 handful cilantro

Kosher salt and fresh pepper to taste

3 tablespoons olive oil, divided

1 pound small potatoes

2 carrots, sliced

1 small red onion, sliced

1 package (8 ounces) arugula

Lemon wedges and plain yogurt, for serving

1 Preheat oven to 400°F and line a sheet pan with parchment paper; set aside.

2 Fit Chopping Blade in Work Bowl, add chickpeas, baking powder, onions, garlic, cumin, coriander, hot sauce, cilantro, salt and pepper then secure Lid and attach Motor.

3 Process for 20 seconds or until pieces are small.

4 Use some of the olive oil to apply a thin layer of oil to the parchment-lined sheet pan.

5 Using a small ice cream scoop or spoon, scoop 2-inch balls of falafel mixture onto the sheet pan, scatter potatoes, carrots and onions between the falafel balls then drizzle with remaining oil.

6 Sprinkle all sheet pan contents with additional salt and pepper then bake for 25-30 minutes or until brown and edges of falafel are crispy.

7 When baking is complete, remove, garnish as desired and serve with arugula, lemon wedges and yogurt.

Marian's Tip: *To make this recipe ahead of time, prepare the recipe then cover and refrigerate for up to 2 days before baking. Letting the falafel rest also improves the flavor.*

indoor grilled
steak tacos

Makes 4 servings

For the Marinade:

4 whole garlic cloves

4 green onions

1 jalapeño pepper + more for serving

Handful fresh cilantro + more for serving

Juice of 1 lime

1/2 teaspoon ground cumin

Kosher salt and fresh pepper to taste

3 tablespoons vegetable oil

For the Tacos:

1 pound flank steak

Tortillas, red onions, radishes, cilantro, lime and salsa, for serving

1 Fit Chopping Blade in Work Bowl, add all marinade ingredients then secure Lid and attach Motor.

2 Process for 30 seconds or until pieces are small.

3 Place flank steak into a mixing bowl then pour marinade over steak and let marinate for 20 minutes or refrigerate for up to 24 hours.

4 Preheat an indoor grill or panini grill to medium-high heat then place steak on grill for 4 minutes on each side or until desired doneness.

5 When grilling is complete, remove and let stand for 5 minutes then cut into thin slices.

6 Assemble tacos with steak, tortillas, red onions, radishes, cilantro, lime, salsa and additional jalapeño peppers before serving.

You can use chicken instead of steak or even sliced mushrooms for a vegan version. If you dislike cumin, simply substitute it with oregano or another herb. If you dislike cilantro, you can substitute it with green onions or basil leaves.

Marian's Tip:

cinnamon swirl snack cake

Makes 9 squares

3/4 cup unsalted butter, softened

4 ounces cream cheese, softened

1 1/2 cups granulated sugar

3 large eggs

1 teaspoon vanilla extract

1 1/2 cups all purpose flour

1/2 teaspoon kosher salt

1/4 cup brown sugar

1 1/2 teaspoons ground cinnamon

1. Preheat oven to 325°F and apply nonstick baking spray to a baking dish; set aside.

2. Fit Chopping Blade in Work Bowl, add butter, cream cheese and granulated sugar then secure Lid and attach Motor.

3. Process for 1 minute or until mixture is smooth and fluffy.

4. With the appliance running, pour the eggs and vanilla through the Hopper; process for 5 seconds then stop and scrape down the sides of the Work Bowl using a spatula.

5. Add flour and salt, pulse to combine then scrape into the prepared baking dish.

6. In a small bowl, stir together brown sugar and cinnamon then pour over batter.

7. Bake for 45 minutes or until a wooden pick inserted off-center emerges clean then remove and serve warm.

fish-shaped cheddar crackers

Makes 6 dozen crackers

1 block (8 ounces) extra-sharp Cheddar cheese, cubed

4 tablespoons unsalted butter, cubed

1 cup all purpose flour

1 teaspoon kosher salt + more for sprinkling

1/2 teaspoon onion powder

Pinch of cayenne pepper (optional)

2 tablespoons carrot juice or water

1 Preheat oven to 350°F and line two sheet pans with parchment paper; set aside.

2 Fit Chopping Blade in Work Bowl, add all ingredients, except carrot juice or water, then secure Lid and attach Motor.

3 Process for 10 seconds or until pieces are small.

4 With the appliance running, pour carrot juice or water through the Hopper; process for a few seconds or until a dough ball forms.

5 Roll out the dough between two sheets of plastic wrap until 1/8-inch thick.

6 Cut dough using fish-shaped cookie cutters then place on prepared sheet pans and sprinkle with additional salt.

7 Bake for 15 minutes, rotating sheet pans halfway through baking.

8 Crackers are done when edges just begin to turn brown and crackers are slightly domed.

9 When baking is complete, remove, let cool and serve.

diner-style burgers

Makes 2 burgers

For the Burgers:

10 ounces beef chuck, cut into 1-inch pieces

1 tablespoon vegetable oil

Kosher salt and fresh pepper to taste

2 American cheese slices

Buns, for serving

For the Sauce:

1/4 cup mayonnaise

1 tablespoon ketchup

2 teaspoons yellow mustard

2 teaspoons sweet relish

2 teaspoons yellow onions, minced

1. Fit Chopping Blade in Work Bowl, add half of the beef then secure Lid and attach Motor.

2. Pulse 10 times or until coarsely ground then shape into a burger patty and set aside.

3. Repeat with remaining beef.

4. Preheat the oil in a large skillet over medium-high heat then add the patties.

5. Cook for 2 minutes without moving the patties, press down using a spatula to slightly flatten patties then season with salt and pepper.

6. Flip over, top each patty with a cheese slice, cover with a lid then cook for an additional 1-2 minutes or until desired doneness is achieved and cheese is melted.

7. Remove patties and place on buns.

8. Attach Wire Whisk to Motor, pour all sauce ingredients into the Mixing Beaker then whisk until combined.

9. Top each burger patty with some of the sauce before serving.

chimichurri pork chop bake

Makes 2 servings

For the Pork Chop Bake:

2 zucchini

2 yellow squash

1 medium yellow onion, chunked

2 pork chops, raw

For the Chimichurri Sauce:

Kosher salt and fresh pepper to taste

1 handful each fresh parsley, cilantro and oregano

1 teaspoon honey

1/4 cup red wine vinegar

1/4 cup olive oil

4 whole garlic cloves

1. Preheat oven to 450°F and line a sheet pan with aluminum foil; set aside.

2. Fit Dicer in Work Bowl, secure Lid then attach Motor.

3. Fit as many zucchini, squash and onion pieces as will fit inside the Hopper, process until diced then repeat with remaining zucchini, squash and onions.

4. Transfer diced vegetables to prepared sheet pan then place pork chops on top of the diced vegetables; set aside.

5. Attach Blending Rod to Motor.

6. Place all chimichurri ingredients into the Mixing Beaker, blend until fairly smooth then pour half of the chimichurri over the sheet pan contents and reserve the other half.

7. Season sheet pan contents with additional salt and pepper then bake for 25 minutes or until brown and internal temperature of pork registers 145°F on a meat thermometer.

8. Remove and serve with reserved chimichurri.

homemade fruit roll snack

Makes 12 rolls

1 quart fresh strawberries
2 tablespoons sugar or other sweetener

1. Preheat oven to 200°F and line two sheet pans with parchment paper.

2. Apply nonstick cooking spray to the parchment paper then set aside.

3. Attach Blending Rod to Motor.

4. Place all ingredients into the Mixing Beaker.

5. Puree the strawberries using an up and down motion.

6. Divide mixture between the two sheet pans then spread out evenly almost to the edges.

7. Bake for 4 hours, rotating pans halfway through baking, or until just dry to the touch.

8. When baking is complete, remove and let cool for 10 minutes.

9. Cut into desired lengths using scissors while keeping the parchment attached.

10. Roll each piece into a cylinder, keeping the parchment on the exterior.

11. Store at room temperature in an airtight container for up to two weeks.

easy banana bread

Makes 1 loaf

2 large eggs
1/2 cup unsalted butter, softened
1 cup granulated sugar
4 large overripe bananas
1 teaspoon vanilla extract
2 tablespoons sour cream

2 cups all purpose flour
1 teaspoon baking soda
1/2 teaspoon baking powder
1/2 teaspoon kosher salt
1/2 cup pecans

1   Preheat oven to 350°F and line a loaf pan with parchment paper; set aside.

2   Fit Chopping Blade in Work Bowl, add eggs, butter, sugar, bananas, vanilla and sour cream then secure Lid and attach Motor.

3   Process for 20 seconds or until smooth.

4   Add remaining ingredients, except pecans, to the Work Bowl then pulse just until no dry ingredients are visible.

5   When processing is complete, pour mixture into the prepared loaf pan then top with pecans.

6   Bake for 1 hour or until cracked down the center and a wooden pick inserted off-center emerges clean.

7   Remove and serve hot, warm or at room temperature.

hearty chili

Makes 4 servings

5 whole garlic cloves

1 large yellow onion, chunked

1 large bell pepper, chunked

1 jalapeño pepper, halved, or to taste

2 tablespoons vegetable oil

1 pound ground beef

1 can (28 ounces) diced tomatoes

1 can (15 ounces) dark red kidney beans, drained

2 tablespoons chili powder

Kosher salt and fresh pepper to taste

1 1/2 cups jarred salsa

1 cup beef stock

Corn tortilla chips, sour cream and shredded Cheddar cheese, for serving

1 Fit Chopping Blade in Work Bowl, add garlic, onions, bell peppers and jalapeño pepper then secure Lid and attach Motor.

2 Pulse 20 times or until pieces are small.

3 Preheat the oil in a stockpot over medium-high heat.

4 Transfer the Work Bowl contents to the stockpot then stir for 2-3 minutes or until softened.

5 Add the beef to the stockpot then break up into chunks and cook until beef is no longer pink.

6 Add remaining ingredients, except tortilla chips, sour cream and cheese then stir to combine.

7 When mixture comes to a boil, reduce heat to a simmer.

8 Simmer for 30 minutes, stirring frequently.

9 When cooking is complete, serve with tortilla chips, sour cream and cheese.

Marian's Tip: *For a plant-based or vegan version of this recipe, omit the beef and add 1 package (8 ounces) white mushrooms to step 1, use vegetable stock instead of beef stock, and top with vegan sour cream and vegan cheese.*

low carb almond bread for one

Makes 1 slice

1 large egg

1 tablespoon butter or coconut oil, melted

3 tablespoons almond flour, finely ground

1/4 teaspoon baking powder

Pinch of salt

1/4 teaspoon xanthan gum (optional)

1 teaspoon everything bagel seasoning blend + more for topping

1 Apply nonstick cooking spray to a microwave-safe 4-inch round silicone mold.

2 Attach Wire Whisk to Motor.

3 Crack the egg into the Mixing Beaker.

4 Whip egg for 30 seconds or until tripled in volume.

5 Add remaining ingredients and whisk for an additional 10-15 seconds just to combine.

6 Pour mixture into prepared mold, top with additional everything bagel seasoning blend then microwave for 90 seconds or until puffed.

7 Remove and use as desired.

oatmeal banana baby food

Makes 2 cups

1/2 cup old fashioned oatmeal, uncooked

1 1/2 cups water

1 ripe banana

1 In a large sauce pan over medium heat, combine the oatmeal and water then bring to a simmer.

2 Continue simmering for 20-25 minutes or until very soft.

3 Remove from heat and let cool.

4 Attach Blending Rod to Motor.

5 Add oatmeal and banana to the Mixing Beaker.

6 Blend for 1 minute or until mostly smooth.

7 When blending is complete, serve desired amount immediately.

8 Baby food keeps refrigerated for up to 2 days.

To make different flavored baby foods, replace the banana with your desired soft or ripe fruit such as 1/2 cup blueberries or 1 peach.

Marian's Tip:

71

low carb cloud bread

Makes 4 servings

3 large egg whites	3 tablespoons cream cheese, warmed
1/4 teaspoon cream of tartar	1/4 teaspoon kosher salt
3 large eggs yolks	1/4 teaspoon garlic powder (optional)

1 Preheat oven to 300°F and line a sheet pan with parchment paper.

2 Apply nonstick cooking spray to the parchment paper then set aside.

3 Attach Wire Whisk to Motor.

4 In a mixing bowl, whisk egg whites and cream of tartar for 1 minute or until stiff peaks form then set aside.

5 Place the egg yolks, cream cheese, salt and garlic powder into the Mixing Beaker then whisk for 10 seconds or until uniform.

6 Fold the Mixing Beaker contents into the egg whites using a spatula.

7 Divide mixture into four mounds on the prepared sheet pan then smooth out the tops using the spatula.

8 Bake for 30 minutes or until puffed and brown.

9 When baking is complete, remove and use as desired.

Marian's Tip: *To add a lovely crispiness to the exterior, put into a toaster before serving. Also, this bread freezes beautifully between sheets of parchment paper in a plastic zipper top bag for up to 2 months without any loss of flavor.*

oven fried rice

Makes 4 servings

1 medium yellow onion, chunked

1 carrot, chunked

1 cup broccoli florets

6 green onions

1 cup white mushrooms

3 tablespoons vegetable oil

3 cups leftover cooked rice

1/4 cup soy sauce, or to taste

1 tablespoon rice vinegar

4 ounces diced ham (optional)

1/2 cup frozen peas

2 eggs, beaten

1 Preheat oven to 450°F and apply nonstick cooking spray to a sheet pan; set aside.

2 Fit Dicer in Work Bowl, secure Lid then attach Motor.

3 Fit as many onions, carrots, broccoli, green onions and mushrooms as will fit inside the Hopper and process until diced.

4 Repeat with remaining onions, carrots, broccoli, green onions and mushrooms then transfer all diced vegetables to a large mixing bowl.

5 Add all remaining ingredients, except beaten eggs, to the mixing bowl then stir to combine.

6 Spread mixing bowl contents in an even layer onto the prepared sheet pan then bake for 20 minutes, stirring occasionally.

7 Drizzle beaten egg over fried rice, stir then bake for an additional 5 minutes.

8 When baking is complete, remove and serve hot.

skillet pasta with turkey sausage

Makes 4 servings

4 whole garlic cloves

1 large yellow onion, chunked

1 carrot

1 celery stalk

1 tablespoon vegetable oil

1 package (9.5 ounces) cooked turkey sausage, crumbled

Kosher salt and fresh pepper to taste

4 cups chicken stock

1 jar (4 ounces) sun-dried tomatoes

2 1/2 cups tube pasta, uncooked

1 bag (8 ounces) baby spinach

1/4 cup Parmesan cheese, grated

1 Fit Slicer in Work Bowl, secure Lid then attach Motor.

2 Fit as many garlic, onions, carrot and celery as will fit inside the Hopper and process until sliced.

3 Repeat with remaining garlic, onions, carrot and celery.

4 Preheat a large skillet over medium-high heat, add the oil and Work Bowl contents then stir for 2-3 minutes or until vegetables begin to soften.

5 Add all remaining ingredients, except spinach and Parmesan, stir to combine then cover skillet and simmer for 10-12 minutes. Stir frequently until pasta is tender and sauce has thickened.

6 Stir in the spinach and Parmesan cheese just until spinach wilts then remove from heat and serve.

chocolate cream pie

Makes one pie

1 tablespoon vanilla extract
2 1/2 cups heavy cream, cold
1 cup powdered sugar
4 tablespoons cocoa powder

1 Classic Pie Crust, baked (see page 43)
1/2 cup mini chocolate chips
1/4 cup chocolate sprinkles, for topping

1 Attach Wire Whisk to Motor.

2 Pour the vanilla, heavy cream and powdered sugar into the Mixing Beaker.

3 Whisk for 1 minute or until soft peaks form then set aside 1/3 of the whipped cream.

4 Add the cocoa powder to the remaining 2/3 whipped cream in the Mixing Beaker.

5 Whisk for an additional 10 seconds or just until combined.

6 Pour chocolate mixture into the pie crust then smooth the top using a spatula.

7 Scatter mini chocolate chips across the pie, cover chocolate chips with reserved whipped cream then top with chocolate sprinkles.

8 Cover and refrigerate for a minimum of 2 hours or up to 24 hours before serving.

mousse in a minute

Makes 4 servings

1 cup semi-sweet chocolate chips

2 cups heavy cream, cold

1 cup powdered sugar

2 teaspoons vanilla extract

4 store-bought brownies

12 crispy chocolate wafer cookies

1/2 cup mini chocolate chips

Maraschino cherries (optional)

1 Place semi-sweet chocolate chips into a microwave-safe bowl then microwave in 30-second intervals until melted; set aside to cool.

2 Attach Wire Whisk to Motor.

3 Pour the heavy cream, powdered sugar and vanilla into the Mixing Beaker.

4 Whip mixture for 30 seconds or until soft peaks form.

5 Whisk the cooled chocolate into the cream mixture until just combined.

6 Layer mousse, brownies, cookies and mini chocolate chips in a serving dish.

7 Top with cherries if desired and serve.

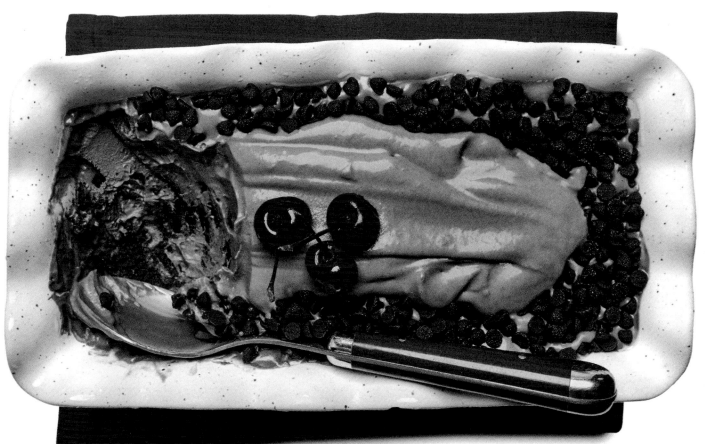

skillet mexican spaghetti

Makes 6 servings

1 bell pepper, chunked

1 medium yellow onion, chunked

8 whole garlic cloves

1 tablespoon vegetable oil

1 pound ground turkey or beef

1 envelope (1 ounce) taco seasoning, or to taste

1 jar (15.5 ounces) salsa

2 cups water

8 ounces broken spaghetti noodles, uncooked

1 cup frozen corn

Kosher salt and fresh pepper to taste

1 cup Mexican cheese blend, shredded

Fresh cilantro and crushed tortilla chips, for serving

1 Fit Slicer in Work Bowl, secure Lid then attach Motor.

2 Fit as many bell peppers, onions and garlic as will fit inside the Hopper and process until sliced.

3 Repeat with remaining bell peppers, onions and garlic.

4 Preheat a large skillet over medium-high heat, add the oil and sliced vegetables then cook for 2-3 minutes or until vegetables begin to soften. Add ground turkey or beef and stir for several minutes until meat is broken up and no longer pink.

5 Add taco seasoning, salsa, water and noodles to the skillet; stir then cover skillet and let simmer for 10 minutes or until pasta is tender and sauce has thickened.

6 Add corn, salt, pepper and cheese then stir until cheese is melted.

7 When cooking is complete, remove, top with cilantro and serve with tortilla chips.

pan-seared
halibut and potatoes

Makes 4 servings

1 pound baby red potatoes

1 medium yellow onion, chunked

2 zucchini

2 tablespoons olive oil

Kosher salt and fresh pepper to taste

4 halibut fillets, cubed

3 tablespoons capers

Zest and juice of 1 lemon

2 tablespoons unsalted butter

1/3 cup chicken stock

1 cup cherry tomatoes, halved

1 Fit Dicer in Work Bowl, secure Lid then attach Motor.

2 Fit as many potatoes, onions and zucchini as will fit inside the Hopper then process until diced.

3 Repeat with remaining potatoes, onions and zucchini.

4 Preheat a large skillet over medium-high heat then add the oil.

5 Add Work Bowl contents to the skillet then season with salt and pepper.

6 Cook for 6-8 minutes, stirring occasionally, or until potatoes are beginning to soften.

7 Add remaining ingredients, except tomatoes, season with additional salt and pepper then cover and simmer gently for 5-6 minutes or until fish flakes easily.

8 Add cherry tomatoes then cook for 1 additional minute or until heated through.

9 Remove, garnish as desired and serve.

chicken wrap with toum

Makes 2 servings

For the Toum (Garlic Sauce):

5 whole garlic cloves

1/2 Fresno chile (optional)

2 tablespoons fresh lemon juice

2 tablespoons water

1/2 teaspoon kosher salt

1 cup vegetable oil

For the Wrap:

2 large flour tortillas

2 garlic ginger chicken breasts, cooked (see recipe on page 57)

1 cup lettuce, shredded

1/4 cucumber, sliced

1/4 cup Feta cheese, crumbled

1 tomato, sliced

1 Attach Blending Rod to Motor.

2 Place all Toum ingredients into the Mixing Beaker.

3 Position the Blending Rod all the way at the bottom of the Mixing Beaker, making sure that all garlic cloves and chile (if using) are positioned under the head of the Blending Rod.

4 While holding the Blending Rod in place at the bottom of the Mixing Beaker, blend for 30 seconds on HIGH speed or until a thick sauce is forming at the bottom of the Mixing Beaker.

5 While continuing to blend, slowly raise the Blending Rod to the top until all oil is incorporated; set aside.

6 Spread two tablespoons Toum on each tortilla then divide remaining wrap ingredients between the tortillas.

7 Roll up each tortilla in a burrito-style fashion.

8 Garnish as desired and serve with additional Toum.

9 Leftover Toum will keep for 1 week in the refrigerator.

When making the Toum, don't be tempted to add extra chile as this emulsified sauce is fragile. Adding extra chile will cause the sauce to appear curdled and become watery within a few hours.

Marian's Tip:

pasta
frittata

Makes 4 servings

1 small yellow onion, chunked

1/4 cup pepperoncini peppers

2 whole garlic cloves

1 handful fresh basil leaves

1/2 red bell pepper, chunked

Kosher salt and fresh pepper to taste

6 large eggs, beaten

1/2 cup Parmesan cheese, grated

1/2 cup Prosciutto or ham, sliced

2 cups spaghetti or other pasta, cooked

3 tablespoons olive oil

Fresh chives, for serving

1 Preheat oven to 375°F then apply nonstick cooking spray to a casserole dish.

2 Fit Slicer in Work Bowl, secure Lid then attach Motor.

3 Fit as many onions as will fit inside the Hopper and process until sliced.

4 Repeat with remaining onions, pepperoncini, garlic, basil and bell peppers.

5 Transfer Work Bowl contents to a mixing bowl then add remaining ingredients, except chives.

6 Pour mixing bowl contents into prepared casserole dish.

7 Bake for 20-25 minutes or until browned, puffy and just set.

8 When baking is complete, remove, garnish with chives and serve hot.

kale and cranberry salad

Makes 4 servings

10 kale leaves

4 green onions

1 carrot

1/4 red bell pepper

1 cup seedless green grapes

1/4 cup apple cider vinegar

1/4 cup honey

1/4 cup olive oil

Kosher salt and fresh pepper to taste

1/4 cup dried cranberries

1/4 cup sunflower seeds

1 Fit Slicer in Work Bowl, secure Lid then attach Motor.

2 Stand as many kale leaves as will fit inside the Hopper and process until sliced.

3 Repeat with remaining kale leaves, green onions, carrot, bell pepper and grapes then set aside.

4 To make the dressing, whisk together the vinegar, honey, olive oil, salt and pepper in a large serving bowl.

5 Add the Work Bowl contents and remaining ingredients to the serving bowl then toss and serve.

sheet pan lamb patties

Makes 4 servings

1/2 cup pistachio nuts

1 large yellow onion, chunked

3 whole garlic cloves

1 handful fresh mint

1 handful fresh cilantro

1 pound ground lamb

1 tablespoon fresh lemon juice

2 tablespoons olive oil, divided

1 bag (12 ounces) frozen peas

1 handful fresh oregano leaves

Kosher salt and fresh pepper to taste

Lemon wedges and plain yogurt, for serving

Marian's Tip: *Make this recipe with half beef and half lamb if you are not sure if you like the taste of lamb.*

1 Preheat oven to 450°F.

2 Fit Chopping Blade in Work Bowl, add nuts, onions, garlic, mint, cilantro, lamb and lemon juice then secure Lid and attach Motor.

3 Process for 20 seconds or until pieces are small.

4 Use some of the olive oil to apply a thin layer of oil to a sheet pan.

5 Using a small ice cream scoop or spoon, scoop 2-inch balls of lamb mixture onto the sheet pan, spacing them out evenly. Pat down each ball into a patty.

6 Bake for 15 minutes then remove pan and flip patties over.

7 Scatter peas and oregano between the patties then drizzle with remaining oil.

8 Sprinkle all sheet pan contents with salt and pepper then place in the oven.

9 Bake for an additional 10 minutes or until edges of patties are crispy or until desired doneness.

10 When baking is complete, remove and serve with lemon wedges and yogurt.

vegetarian enchiladas

Makes 4 servings

2 packages (8 ounces each) mushrooms

1 large yellow onion, chunked

6 whole garlic cloves

1 jalapeño pepper, halved (optional)

1 handful fresh cilantro + more for topping

2 tablespoons vegetable oil

Kosher salt and fresh pepper to taste

12 corn tortillas, warmed

1 can (28 ounces) enchilada sauce

2 cups Cheddar cheese, shredded

1 Preheat oven to 350°F and apply nonstick cooking spray to a sheet pan.

2 Fit Chopping Blade in Work Bowl, add mushrooms, onions, garlic, jalapeño peppers and cilantro then secure Lid and attach Motor.

3 Pulse 15-20 times or until pieces are small.

4 Preheat the oil in a large skillet over medium-high heat.

5 Add Work Bowl contents to the skillet, season with salt and pepper, cook and stir for 5-6 minutes or until vegetables are softened then remove from heat.

6 On a work surface, lay out a few tortillas at a time, spoon a line of mushroom mixture down the center of each tortilla then roll up.

7 Place seam-side down on the sheet pan, repeat with remaining tortillas and mushroom mixture then pour enchilada sauce evenly over the sheet pan contents.

8 Top with cheese then bake in the center of the oven for 30 minutes or until bubbly.

9 When baking is complete, remove, top with additional cilantro and serve.

real ranch dressing

Makes 1 1/2 cups

2 whole garlic cloves
1/4 medium yellow onion
4 green onions
Handful of fresh parsley
Handful of fresh dill

Kosher salt and fresh pepper to taste
1/2 cup mayonnaise
1/2 cup whole milk
2 tablespoons apple cider vinegar

1 Fit Chopping Blade in Work Bowl, add all ingredients then secure Lid and attach Motor.

2 Process for 30 seconds or until thick and mostly smooth.

3 When processing is complete, transfer to an airtight storage container.

4 Keeps refrigerated for up to 2 weeks.

While the ingredient list seems long, this is a very simple recipe to prepare as this wonderful appliance does all the work with ease. The end result is well worth it compared to bottled store-bought Ranch dressing.

Marian's Tip:

gooey cinnamon monkey bread

Makes 6 servings

2 cups mini marshmallows

1 cup granulated sugar

1/2 cup unsalted butter, melted

2 tablespoons ground cinnamon

1 tablespoon vanilla extract

Pinch of kosher salt

1 ball store-bought pizza dough (1 pound)

1   Apply nonstick baking spray to a bundt pan and set aside.

2   Fit Chopping Blade in Work Bowl, add all ingredients, except pizza dough, then secure Lid and attach Motor.

3   Process for 30 seconds or until combined then remove Chopping Blade and set aside.

4   Cut pizza dough into golf ball-size pieces.

5   Dip each dough piece in cinnamon mixture in the Work Bowl then transfer to the prepared pan.

6   Repeat until all dough pieces are coated and placed in the pan. It is not necessary to arrange the dough pieces in any particular order as they will all knit together during baking.

7   Cover with plastic wrap and let rise for 40 minutes or until doubled in bulk.

8   Preheat oven to 350°F while dough is rising.

9   Bake for 40-50 minutes or until brown and a thermometer inserted in the center registers 195°F.

10 When baking is complete, remove and let rest for 10 minutes before removing from pan.

11 Serve hot or warm.

japanese
puffy pancakes

Makes 2 large pancakes

1 1/2 cups all purpose flour

3 tablespoons powdered sugar

2 teaspoons baking powder

1/2 teaspoon kosher salt

1 1/4 cups whole milk

4 tablespoons unsalted butter, melted

1/2 teaspoon vanilla extract

1 large egg yolk

3 large egg whites

1/4 teaspoon cream of tartar

Syrup and butter, for serving

1   Fit Chopping Blade in Work Bowl, add flour, powdered sugar, baking powder and salt then secure Lid and attach Motor.

2   Process for 5 seconds to combine.

3   With the appliance running, pour the milk, melted butter, vanilla and egg yolk through the Hopper and process for 5 seconds or just until combined; remove Chopping Blade then set Work Bowl aside.

4   Attach Wire Whisk to Motor.

5   Place the egg whites and cream of tartar into the Mixing Beaker.

6   Whip egg whites for 1 minute or until stiff peaks form.

7   Fold egg whites into the Work Bowl contents using a spatula.

8   Preheat a 10-inch nonstick pan over medium-low heat and apply nonstick cooking spray to the pan.

9   Spoon half of the batter into the pan then cover with lid.

10 Cook for 3-4 minutes or until bottom of pancake is brown (check occasionally to prevent over-browning).

11 Carefully flip pancake over, cover then cook for an additional 3-4 minutes or until other side of pancake is brown.

12 Remove and repeat with remaining batter.

13 Serve with syrup and butter.

Marian's Tip: *This recipe is easy to make gluten-free without changing the taste. Simply substitute 1 1/2 cups gluten-free baking mix for the flour in this recipe.*

carrot cake

Makes 1 cake

2 large carrots, chunked	1 teaspoon ground cinnamon
1/2 cup pineapple, chunked	2 cups all purpose flour
2 large eggs	1 teaspoon baking soda
1/2 cup vegetable oil	1 teaspoon baking powder
1 1/3 cups granulated sugar	1 teaspoon vanilla extract
1 1/2 teaspoons kosher salt	1 can (16 ounces) cream cheese frosting

1. Preheat oven to 350°F and apply nonstick baking spray to a tube pan; set aside.

2. Fit Chopping Blade in Work Bowl, add carrots and pineapple then secure Lid and attach Motor.

3. Process for 1 minute or until pureed.

4. Add remaining ingredients, except frosting, pulse to combine then transfer to the prepared pan.

5. Bake for 1 hour or until a wooden pick inserted in the center emerges clean.

6. When baking is complete, remove and let cool completely.

7. Cover top of the cake with frosting and serve.

cinnamon
peanut butter schmear

About 1 cup

1/4 cup unsalted butter, melted
1 teaspoon ground cinnamon
2/3 cup natural peanut butter, chunky or smooth
4 tablespoons honey

1   Attach Wire Whisk to Motor.

2   Pour all ingredients into the Mixing Beaker.

3   Whisk for 30 seconds or until combined.

4   Transfer to an airtight storage container.

5   Schmear keeps in the refrigerator for up to 1 week.

chicken marsala dinner

Makes 2 servings

1 pound small potatoes

1 medium yellow onion, chunked

1 package (8 ounces) white mushrooms

2 chicken breasts, raw

1/2 cup all purpose flour

Kosher salt and fresh pepper to taste

2 tablespoons olive oil, divided

2/3 cup marsala wine

2/3 cup chicken stock

2 tablespoons unsalted butter

4 sage leaves

1 Fit Slicer in Work Bowl, secure Lid then attach Motor.

2 Fit as many potatoes, onions and mushrooms as will fit inside the Hopper and process until sliced.

3 Repeat with remaining potatoes, onions and mushrooms then set aside.

4 Dredge chicken in flour then season with salt and pepper; shake off excess flour.

5 Preheat a large skillet over medium-high heat then add 1 tablespoon oil.

6 Place chicken in the skillet, cook for 4 minutes on each side then remove.

7 Add remaining oil and Work Bowl contents to the skillet then season with additional salt and pepper.

8 Cook for 6-8 minutes, stirring frequently, or until potatoes are tender.

9 Return chicken and remaining ingredients to the skillet, bring to a simmer then cook for 5 minutes or until chicken is cooked through and sauce is beginning to thicken.

10 When cooking is complete, remove, garnish as desired and serve.

For a different variation, add 8 ounces of angel hair pasta in step 9, increase the stock to 2 cups then cover and increase the cooking time to 6-7 minutes or until pasta is tender.

Marian's Tip:

scalloped potatoes

Makes 4 servings

4 large Yukon Gold potatoes, cut to fit inside the Hopper

2 cups heavy cream

2 teaspoons kosher salt or to taste

1 tablespoon fresh chives, chopped

1. Preheat oven to 350°F and apply nonstick cooking spray to a baking dish; set aside.

2. Fit Slicer in Work Bowl, secure Lid then attach Motor.

3. Fit as many potatoes as will fit inside the Hopper and process until sliced.

4. Repeat with remaining potatoes.

5. Pour cream and salt over the sliced potatoes inside the Work Bowl then toss using a spatula until all potato slices are evenly coated.

6. Transfer Work Bowl contents to the prepared baking dish.

7. Bake for 45 minutes or until brown, bubbly and potatoes are fork tender.

8. When baking is complete, remove, top with chives and serve.

seven layer salad

Makes 6 servings

For the Salad:

2 romaine lettuce heads

1 celery stalk

1 small yellow onion, chunked

2 cups frozen peas, thawed

1 1/2 cups Cheddar cheese, shredded

1 package (3.5 ounces) cooked, chopped bacon

For the Dressing:

1 cup mayonnaise

2 tablespoons yellow mustard

2 tablespoons granulated sugar

1 tablespoon apple cider vinegar

Kosher salt and fresh pepper to taste

1. Fit Slicer in Work Bowl, secure Lid then attach Motor.

2. Stand as many lettuce leaves as will fit inside the Hopper and process until sliced.

3. Repeat with remaining lettuce then transfer to a serving dish.

4. Using the Hopper, process the celery and onions until sliced, place on top of lettuce inside the serving dish then pat down into an even layer.

5. Top with peas then pat down into an even layer.

6. Attach Wire Whisk to Motor, pour all dressing ingredients into the Mixing Beaker, whisk until smooth then pour over the peas in the serving dish and spread into an even layer.

7. Top with cheese and bacon then cover with plastic wrap and refrigerate for a minimum of 1 hour or up to 1 day before serving.

layered taco dip

Makes 8 servings

1 large yellow onion, chunked

1 tablespoon vegetable oil

1 pound lean ground beef

1 package (1 ounce) taco seasoning, or to taste

4 Roma tomatoes

1 can (16 ounces) refried beans

1 cup sour cream

1 cup Cheddar cheese, shredded

1 avocado, diced

1/3 cup sliced black olives

Handful of fresh cilantro leaves

Tortilla chips, for serving

1 Fit Dicer in Work Bowl, secure Lid then attach Motor.

2 Fit as many onions, as will fit inside the Hopper, process until diced then repeat with remaining onions.

3 Preheat a large skillet over medium-high heat then add oil.

4 Add onions and beef, stir for 3-5 minutes or until beef is no longer pink then stir in the taco seasoning; remove from heat.

5 Fit as many tomatoes, as will fit inside the Hopper, process until diced then repeat with remaining tomatoes.

6 Spread the refried beans into the bottom of a shallow serving dish.

7 Top beans with beef mixture, tomatoes, sour cream, cheese, avocados, olives and cilantro then serve with tortilla chips.

easy microwave pasta alfredo

Makes 2 servings

4 whole garlic cloves

1/2 cup Parmesan cheese, grated + more for serving

1 green onion

Kosher salt and fresh pepper to taste

1/4 cup unsalted butter, softened

1/2 cup heavy cream

Cooked pasta or zoodles of your choice

1 Fit Chopping Blade in Work Bowl, add all ingredients, except cream and pasta or zoodles, then secure Lid and attach Motor.

2 Process for 30 seconds or until smooth.

3 With the appliance running, pour the cream through the Hopper and process just until mostly smooth (do not over process).

4 Transfer mixture to a microwave-safe dish then microwave for 3-4 minutes or until hot and bubbly.

5 Stir, toss in the pasta or zoodles then microwave for an additional 1-2 minutes or until heated through.

6 Top with additional Parmesan cheese, garnish as desired and serve.

one skillet chicken scampi

Makes 2 servings

1 medium yellow onion, chunked

1 red bell pepper, chunked

8 whole garlic cloves

1 pound chicken tenders, raw

Kosher salt and fresh pepper to taste

1/4 cup white wine

1 cup heavy cream

Juice of 1 lemon

1/4 cup parsley, chopped

Cooked pasta, for serving

1 Fit Slicer in Work Bowl, secure Lid then attach Motor.

2 Fit as many onions, bell peppers and garlic cloves as will fit inside the Hopper and process until sliced.

3 Repeat with remaining onions, bell peppers and garlic cloves then transfer to a large skillet.

4 Add remaining ingredients, except parsley and pasta, to the skillet then bring to a boil over high heat.

5 Reduce temperature to a simmer then stir constantly for 5 minutes or until sauce has thickened and chicken is cooked through.

6 When cooking is complete, remove, top with parsley, garnish as desired and serve over pasta.

deviled egg dip

Makes 8 servings

8 hard-boiled eggs
1/2 cup mayonnaise or to taste
4 ounces cream cheese, softened
3 tablespoons sweet pickle relish
2 tablespoons yellow mustard

1 green onion
Kosher salt and fresh pepper to taste
Paprika, for topping
Dippers of your choice, for serving

1 Attach Masher to Motor.

2 Place all ingredients, except paprika and dippers, into a large mixing bowl.

3 Mash mixing bowl contents until desired texture is achieved.

4 When mashing is complete, transfer to a serving bowl.

5 Sprinkle with paprika and serve with your favorite dippers.

chocolate
loaf cake

Makes 1 cake

1 cup (2 sticks) unsalted butter, softened

2 cups light brown sugar, packed

1/2 cup cocoa powder

1 cup boiling water

2 teaspoons vanilla extract

3 large eggs

2 cups all purpose flour

1 teaspoon baking powder

1 1/2 teaspoons kosher salt

1 cup semi-sweet chocolate chips

Powdered sugar, for serving

1 Preheat oven to 350°F and apply nonstick baking spray to a loaf pan; set aside.

2 Fit Chopping Blade in Work Bowl, add butter, sugar, cocoa powder, water, vanilla and eggs then secure Lid and attach Motor.

3 Process for 30 seconds or until mostly smooth.

4 Add the flour, baking powder and salt then pulse until no flour remains visible.

5 Using a spatula, stir in the chocolate chips then pour batter into the prepared loaf pan.

6 Bake for 40-50 minutes or until a wooden pick inserted off-center emerges with just a few moist crumbs clinging to it (cake will sink slightly in center).

7 When baking is complete, let cool for 10 minutes then remove from pan.

8 Sprinkle with powdered sugar and serve.

confetti dessert dip

Makes 2 1/2 cups

1 package (8 ounces) cream cheese, softened
1 tub (8 ounces) whipped topping, thawed
1 cup powdered sugar
1/2 teaspoon cake batter extract (optional)

1/2 cup confetti sprinkles
Dippers of your choice

1. Place cream cheese in a large mixing bowl.
2. Attach Wire Whisk to Motor.
3. Blend cream cheese for 30 seconds or until smooth.
4. Add whipped topping, powdered sugar, extract and confetti sprinkles.
5. Mix for an additional 30 seconds or until uniform.
6. Transfer to a serving dish, garnish as desired and serve with dippers.

easy chicken bolognese

Makes 6 servings

1 large yellow onion, chunked

1 large carrot, chunked

1 celery stalk, chunked

4 whole garlic cloves

1 pound boneless, skinless chicken thighs

1 tablespoon unsalted butter

2 tablespoons tomato paste

1/2 cup water

Kosher salt and fresh pepper to taste

1/2 cup dry white wine

1 cup chicken stock

1 can (14 ounces) diced tomatoes

1 sprig fresh rosemary

Cooked pasta and ricotta cheese, for serving

1   Fit Chopping Blade in Work Bowl, add onions, carrots, celery, garlic and chicken then secure Lid and attach Motor.

2   Process for 15-20 seconds or until pieces are small.

3   Preheat a large saucepan over medium heat and add the butter.

4   Add the Work Bowl contents to the saucepan and cook for 5-10 minutes, stirring frequently, or until chicken is cooked through.

5   Add remaining ingredients, except pasta and ricotta cheese, to the saucepan.

6   Cook for an additional 20-30 minutes or until slightly thick and bubbly.

7   When cooking is complete, pour over pasta then top with ricotta cheese and additional pepper before serving.

california roll in a bowl

Makes 2 servings

4 cups cooked sushi rice, cold
2 tablespoons seasoned rice vinegar
1/2 English cucumber
4 green onions
1 carrot

4 ounces real or imitation crab
1 avocado, diced
Soy sauce, pickled ginger, sesame seeds and wasabi, for serving

1 Divide the rice between two large serving bowls then sprinkle with vinegar.

2 Fit Slicer in Work Bowl, secure Lid then attach Motor.

3 Stand cucumber inside the Hopper, process until sliced then divide between the rice bowls.

4 Repeat with green onions and divide between the rice bowls.

5 Fit Shredder in Work Bowl, secure Lid then attach Motor.

6 Fit carrot inside the Hopper, process until shredded then divide between the rice bowls.

7 Divide crab and avocados between the bowls then serve with soy sauce, pickled ginger, sesame seeds and wasabi.

no-boil
stuffed shells

Makes 6 servings

2 whole garlic cloves

1 large egg

1 tub (15 ounces) whole milk ricotta cheese

1 bag (8 ounces) Italian cheese blend, shredded

1 bag (9.5 ounces) cooked sausage crumbles

Kosher salt and fresh pepper to taste

1 box (12 ounces) jumbo pasta shells, uncooked

1 jar (24 ounces) pasta sauce

2 cups water

1 cup mozzarella cheese, shredded

1 Preheat oven to 400°F and apply nonstick cooking spray to a baking dish; set aside.

2 Fit Chopping Blade in Work Bowl, add garlic, egg, ricotta, Italian cheese blend, sausage crumbles, salt and pepper then secure Lid and attach Motor.

3 Pulse for 30 seconds or until well combined.

4 Spoon cheese mixture into a plastic zipper top bag, twist and hold at the top then snip one corner off using scissors to make a piping bag.

5 Pipe mixture into pasta shells.

6 Pour half of the pasta sauce into the bottom of the prepared baking dish.

7 Place shells into the baking dish with cheese-side facing up then top with remaining pasta sauce.

8 Pour water over all baking dish contents then top with mozzarella cheese.

9 Cover baking dish tightly with aluminum foil then bake for 1 hour or until pasta is tender and sauce is bubbly.

10 When baking is complete, remove, garnish as desired and serve hot.

Marian's Tip: *This recipe can be prepared through step 8 up to 2 days ahead of baking. Also, you can prepare this recipe using turkey sausage or even plant-based beefless meat crumbles.*

pizza pull-apart

Makes 6 servings

4 whole garlic cloves

2 sprigs fresh oregano

1 1/2 cups jarred pasta sauce

1/3 cup sun-dried tomatoes, undrained

6 hard salami slices, quartered

1/4 cup olive oil

1/2 cup Parmesan cheese, grated

1 ball store-bought pizza dough (1 pound)

1 package (5 ounces) mini pepperoni slices

2 cups mozzarella cheese, shredded

1. Apply nonstick cooking spray to a large oven-safe skillet and set aside.

2. Fit Chopping Blade in Work Bowl, add garlic, oregano, pasta sauce, sun-dried tomatoes, salami, olive oil and Parmesan cheese then secure Lid and attach Motor.

3. Process for 30 seconds or until combined then remove Chopping Blade and set aside.

4. Cut pizza dough into golf ball-size pieces.

5. Dip each dough piece in sauce mixture in the Work Bowl.

6. Arrange coated dough pieces in a single layer inside the prepared skillet, top with some pepperoni and mozzarella then repeat to make additional layers.

7. Cover with plastic wrap and let rise for 40 minutes or until doubled in bulk.

8. Preheat oven to 350°F while dough is rising then bake for 40-50 minutes or until brown and a thermometer registers 195°F in the center.

9. When baking is complete, remove, let rest for 10 minutes then remove from skillet and serve.

source page

Here are some of my favorite places to find ingredients that are not readily available at grocery stores as well as kitchen tools and supplies that help you become a better cook.

THE BAKERS CATALOGUE AT KING ARTHUR FLOUR

Gel or paste food colorings, pastry bags, baking pans, cake pans, blowtorches, rubber and silicone spatulas, digital timers, kitchen scales, natural parchment paper, the best instant-read thermometers, off-set spatulas, measuring cups and spoons, knives, cookie sheets, jimmies and sprinkles.

www.kingarthurflour.com

WILTON ENTERPRISES

Everything needed for cake decorating. Cake decorating turntables, cake pans, spatulas, cake icer tips, ice cream scoops, colored sugars, gel and paste food coloring, sprinkles, cake scrapers and side smoothers, decorating tips, bundt pans, fish-shaped cookie cutters and baking dishes.

Wilton also sells many of their supplies at Michael's crafts, Jo-Ann crafts and Walmart.

www.wilton.com

AMAZON

Everything bagel seasoning blend, Fish-shaped cookie cutters, kitchen scales, 4-inch round silicone molds, measuring cups and most other cooking and baking supplies.

www.amazon.com

VANILLA FROM TAHITI

My favorite pure vanilla extract and the best quality vanilla beans.

www.vanillafromtahiti.com

WHOLE FOODS

Natural food coloring, natural sprinkles, natural and organic baking ingredients, natural parchment paper, good quality chocolate such as Valhrona and Callebaut.

www.wholefoods.com

KEREKES THE CHEF STATION

All varieties of cake pans, spatulas, cake decorating turntables, cake scrapers, baking pans and cake side smoothers.

www.bakedeco.com

CHOCOSPHERE

Excellent quality cocoa (Callebaut), all Chocolates, Jimmies and sprinkles.

www.chocosphere.com

index